# Table of Contents

# Winston Churchill

---

*A Biography of Historical Icon*

*Winston Churchill*

**Henry Hanson**

# Introduction

Winston Churchill is an iconic figure. Any mention of his name will perhaps conjure the iconic photograph of him taken by a young Yousef Karsh, who never suspected how his 'Roaring Lion' would be known around the world. It shows a dapper but distinguished statesman whose steady gaze conveys something of his intelligence and intensity but also, in some subtle way, his generosity of spirit.

Or, one might think of Ivor Roberts Jones' bronze statue of Churchill that is located in Parliament Square, Westminster, depicting Churchill clad in a heavy military greatcoat with his hand resting on a cane, which is based on a photograph of him inspecting a bomb-damaged Houses of Parliament during the Second World War. Churchill pointed out to his wife the spot where his statue would stand, as he had a sense of his own destiny and that he would earn his place among the most eminent parliamentarians.

There are so many photographs of Churchill crunching resolutely through the rubble of homes and workplaces in an East End of London that was tortured and flattened but unbowed by Luftwaffe raids. Perhaps, one might even picture the rumpled corporeality and chin-jutting stubbornness of the elder statesman in Graham Sutherland's portrait; Churchill hated that one so much that his wife, the loyal Clementine, destroyed it after his death.

Still, others might imagine the gentleman descending from a "flying boat" after a grueling transatlantic flight, or, more leisurely, striding in the garden of his beloved Chartwell clad in one of his extraordinary siren suits in a blurred polaroid. And some may invoke him cutting a dash as a young cavalry officer of the South African Wars.

This book aims to walk through this kaleidoscope of images and build its own portrait of a multi-faceted and fascinating man.

# Chapter 1: Early Life

Winston Churchill began his life in an imposing baroque palace in Oxfordshire, England in the early hours of the morning of November 30, 1874. This was Blenheim Palace, built in 1705, a masterpiece of the architect John Vanburgh that was intended to rival Versailles. It was the home of his grandfather, John Winston Spencer Churchill, the 7th Duke of Marlborough. It was an auspicious and privileged place to start life. Churchill loved Blenheim and spent much time there throughout his life.

He was born at the height of the Victorian era into the English aristocracy and into a family engaged with politics and public life. His parents were Randolph Henry Churchill, a younger son of the family, and Jennie (née Jerome,) an American heiress and socialite.

## Early Years

His early life followed the pattern of an aristocratic childhood of the era. Though growing up in splendid surroundings, he would have had limited interaction with his parents, being principally cared for by servants. His nanny was a woman called Mrs. Everest (nannies were all called "Mrs." even if they were not married). She was a very important figure in Churchill's life. He was by nature an affectionate child and she was the available object for his affections. She accompanied the family on their travels abroad and was the center of Churchill's emotional life. His pet name for her was "Woom" or "Woomany," and he corresponded with her until her death in 1895, which moved him deeply. He subsequently paid for her funerary monument and the upkeep of her grave.

A considerable amount of Churchill's early life was spent in Ireland in a house called Little Lodge. From 1876 to 1880, his grandfather, the 7th Duke of Marlborough, served as the Lord Lieutenant of Ireland, popularly called the viceroy. Churchill would have lived at Dublin Castle during the season and otherwise at a lodge in Dublin's Phoenix Park. Churchill's father accompanied his father as a private secretary.

It is in this environment that Churchill first encountered a governess; he speaks of this in his autobiographical *My Early Life* as something that filled him with dismay. This is the first indication of Churchill's distaste for most of the educational experiences of his young life. There is never any suggestion that he lacked intelligence or ability; rather that he was selective in which subjects and activities could win his attention and that he had a tendency to clash with authority.

At the age of 5, Churchill gained a sibling, John Strange Spencer Churchill, known as Jack, and they were good companions throughout their youth.

## Preparatory Schools

At 7 years old, like others of his social class, Churchill was dispatched to a prep boarding school. Such schools prepared their charges for one of the famous English public schools, ancient private institutions for the rich and privileged. At first, he attended St. James' School in Ascot, Berkshire, where he was deeply unhappy. He was homesick and clashed with his teachers, being strong-willed and disobedient.

The school dispensed harsh punishments, including flogging with birches. His parents, with concerns for his health, sent him to another school on the East Sussex coast at Hove. He was happier at this more liberal establishment run by the Thomson sisters. He was allowed to concentrate on the subjects he enjoyed, including French, English, and horsemanship. A leading actress, who taught dancing at the Brunswick School, considered him the naughtiest boy of her acquaintance. The Thomson sisters managed to elicit the best efforts of Churchill with non-violent management sufficiently for him to be able to pass the entrance exams for Harrow School in 1885.

## Harrow School

Harrow was, and still is, one of the top English Public Schools and boasts several English prime ministers and other leading figures. Harrow has educated boys since the 13th century and was recognized by Royal Charter of Elizabeth I in 1572. Like all public schools, it dispensed a rigorous academic education with a strong emphasis on the classics. Tradition, sportsmanship, and participation in military cadet corps are features of public-school life. There were various arcane traditions, such as the system of fagging (pupils acting as servants to older boys). Harrow and other schools of this type instill a strong sense of national pride and civic duty. Pupils are taught to be aware of their privilege and their duty to serve their country militarily and otherwise. Harrow has a motto *Donorum Dei Dispensatio Fidelis*, which means "the faithful dispensation of the gifts of God," alongside its more famous motto *Stet Fortuna Domus*, which means "Let the fortune of the house stand."

It must have been a comfort to Churchill when his brother joined him at school, and he and Jack were able to share a room. Jack was serious and dedicated to his studies and this highlighted Winston's indifferent performance.

His career at Harrow was not illustrious. He continued to rebel against authority and was frequently in trouble. He particularly hated Latin and later even boasted that "In all the twelve years I was at school, no one ever succeeded in making me write a Latin verse or write any Greek except the alphabet." Ironically, he was later to develop a taste for incorporating Latin quotations into his speeches.

Schooling was a time of misery and isolation for Churchill, who bore it all very stoically. His son wrote his official biography and stated that he believed enduring the misery, punishments, and humiliations of Harrow strengthened him and shaped him as a man. Survival depended on developing resilience and independence. Despite his dogged refusal to work at subjects and activities that did not interest him, he also displayed the ability, on occasion, to show extraordinary focus and concentration. Churchill did shine in English. He once was able to recite 1,200 lines of an epic poem about ancient Rome, and he earned the approbation of his English master, Mr. Somervell. Unfortunately, it was Latin and mathematics that were esteemed at Harrow. He also acquitted himself well as an athlete, tellingly at individual sports, including fencing and swimming, rather than team sports. He was also an able and enthusiastic participant in the Harrow School Rifle Corps, a cadet company within the 18th Middlesex Volunteer Corps. Harrow school students would have been drilled from the first day that they were expected to become leaders of men in the world at large, and military officers if their country needed them.

Churchill felt his parents' neglect keenly throughout his time at school. As a young child, his plaintive letters asking his mother to visit or to allow him to go home were unheeded. During his years at Harrow, his Father visited him only once, and that was only at the behest of the headmaster, and he sent his son only five letters. Churchill wrote to him repeatedly without reply before giving up. When he had been at prep school near Brighton, he learned that his father had been visiting close by and wrote reproachfully to ask why his father had not found time to call on him: "I dare say you are very busy." His mother was slightly more attentive, though was still predominately absent from his life during this time.

Relationships between parents and children among the upper classes were typically distant at this time, with all hands-on care delegated to servants, but Churchill's parents seem particularly disengaged, far too busy with their own lives. Famously, the upper classes felt that affection properly should only be demonstrated towards dogs and horses. Even if it was the custom of time and class, it will have caused an emotional wound. Certainly, Churchill was to crave the attention and approval of his father all of his life. His mother was more affectionate to her sons, but not to the extent of giving them much of her time or attention or of always making decisions with their welfare in mind.

His parents were very open in voicing their disappointment with his scholastic efforts, however, and concluded that he would be unsuited for university life, and so, he bent his ambitions towards a military career, beginning at Sandhurst.

# Sandhurst

Sandhurst is the Royal Military Academy and is the training school for all officers in the British Army. It is located on the borders of Berkshire and Surrey. A physically and mentally demanding program of instruction prepares students to lead soldiers.

Entry to Sandhurst was a stumbling block for Churchill, who had to attempt the civil service entrance exam required three times and even attended a crammer, an intensive training program, in order to prepare for the test. However, he achieved his objective by 1893.

Churchill's poor scoring in the entrance exam meant that he did not qualify for infantry officer training. He thought he would have to enter as a trainee cavalry officer. This was the cause of some consternation at home. A cavalry place would have entailed additional expense for his father, as a cavalry kit was expensive and there was the necessity to supply one's own horses and polo ponies. Fortunately, as another candidate dropped out at the last minute, he was accepted into infantry training by default, not merit.

Churchill's time at Sandhurst was much more to his liking than his school days. He found military strategy interesting, and as an able and keen horseman and fencer, he had the skills to excel. He completed his studies at Sandhurst in 1894, finishing a very creditable 8th out of 150 graduates. This left Churchill free and ambitious to make his mark on the world.

# Chapter 2: Churchill's Parents

## Lord Randolph Churchill

Randolph Henry Spencer Churchill was born in 1849 in Belgravia, London, the third son of the Marquess of Blandford, who became, upon the death of his father, the 7th Duke of Marlborough. As a third son, Randolph Churchill was given the courtesy title of Lord, but was a commoner, thus eligible to sit in the House of Commons. He did aspire to political life, following the example of his forebearers. He was educated at Eton College and Merton College, Oxford, and graduated with a degree in jurisprudence and modern history. His sojourn at Oxford was characterized by riotous and irresponsible behavior and he was frequently in trouble.

Randolph Churchill married the American heiress Jennie Jerome in Paris in 1874 after a whirlwind romance. She was the daughter of an extremely wealthy property developer. It was quite usual at the time for cash-strapped British aristocrats to buoy their fortunes by making financially felicitous marriages with transatlantic heiresses. Wealthy Americans were buying status and titles, and British aristocrats were shoring up their stately homes and funding extravagant lifestyles. However, this particular match was not favored by either set of parents.

Jennie Jerome did not bring nearly as much money as was required, and the third son of a Duke was not a sufficient prize for Jennie's family. Jennie was beautiful, intelligent, and vivacious. They married in April, and Winston Churchill was born in November, apparently prematurely, but this might hint at risqué behavior (for the time) and explain a precipitous and imprudent marriage. In 1874, Randolph Churchill also entered the House of Commons as a member of Parliament for Woodstock in Oxfordshire, so it was quite a year for him.

As a Conservative MP, Randolph Churchill made a great first impression entering the house. He was witty, acerbic, and made impassioned and engaging speeches. His maiden speech was publicly praised by Disraeli, the eminent Victorian politician credited with founding the modern Conservative Party, a colorful figure who served the nation twice as the prime minister. However, he did not show himself to be a steady or reliable hand and the reception of his often quite brilliant speeches was undermined by his erratic moods, behavior, and sometimes quasi-hysterical delivery.

Randolph Churchill quarreled unnecessarily with the Prince of Wales in 1876, about the Prince's amorous indiscretions and some compromising letters. Randolph Churchill then found himself effectively exiled. His father was appointed in 1876 to the position of the Lord Lieutenant in Ireland, having previously declined similar positions. Randolph Churchill was to accompany his father to act as his private secretary, so the family decamped to Dublin, residing at Dublin Castle in the social season and otherwise in adjacent official residence lodges in Phoenix Park.

In 1885, Randolph Churchill was to serve as the Secretary of State for India where he was responsible for a series of rash and imprudent decisions, such as making trade agreements that heavily disadvantaged India, overspending on the military, failing to accumulate reserves to deal with periods of famine, and not investing sufficiently in public services. The most controversial decision of all was to instigate the Anglo-Burmese War that was a costly and prolonged imperialist exercise.

On the domestic front, Randolph Churchill impressed people with his proposal for Tory democracy, promoting a populist face for conservatism. This was required to win against the Liberals with their appeal to the common man and his interests. In 1886, he rose to become the Leader of the House of Commons and then the Chancellor of the Exchequer and seemed on course for a glittering career. His budgetary plans were considered innovative and intelligent. However, he could be abrasive and uncompromising. He made enemies and even his best friends related that, although he could sparkle in company and be extremely entertaining, he would then suddenly be unaccountably rude and alienating.

With an inexplicable lack of judgment, Randolph Churchill resigned from government in protest over a minor issue, expecting to be invited to return. No invitation was forthcoming. He had shot himself in the foot with regards to his political life.

Randolph Churchill's health deteriorated soon after this and he embarked on world travel. He was to assist his friends, the Rothschilds, in overseeing their South African mines (including the nascent De Beers Diamond Company), an enterprise that netted him a large sum of money that he spent traveling in the Far East. The Rothschilds had generously supported Randolph Churchill throughout their association.

Much speculation has been made about the possibility of Randolph Churchill suffering from secondary and tertiary syphilis at the end of his life. It was reported in a scandalous memoir by an Irish-American writer and friend of the rich and famous, *Frank Harris: My Life and Loves*. Certainly, Randolph was treated by a London physician who had expertise in syphilis, a condition that was, at the time, incurable, with the only treatment available being toxic and problematic, including the administration of mercury. It was also known that in his wild youth he frequented prostitutes. This diagnosis would be consistent with some of his erratic behavior and judgment, which were symptoms of advanced syphilis; although, brain tumors and multiple sclerosis can have similar effects. His treatment began in 1876 and may be part of the reason that he was largely estranged from his wife from the 1880s onward. There has never been any suggestion that Jennie Churchill or the children were affected.

Randolph Churchill showed very little interest in his sons, which Winston found extremely painful. He was desperate to win his father's approval, or even attention. It might be considered that much of Churchill's extraordinary drive, ambition, and courage had some root in the desire to prove himself to an indifferent father. Poignantly, Winston Churchill's granddaughter, when interviewed regarding his legacy, said it would have pleased him to be so esteemed by the country he loved, but it would mean even more to him if he knew his father was able to see and appreciate it.

Dying in 1895, ultimately, Randolph Churchill's life was one of unfulfilled promise. Roy Jenkins, in his work on the British Chancellors of the Exchequer, summarized that he was "without rival in attracting so much attention and achieving so little".

## Jennie Jerome, Lady Randolph Churchill

Jennie Jerome, an American heiress, was the daughter of the financier and property developer Leonard Jerome, who was of Huguenot descent. She was traveling with her mother, staying in Paris in 1873, and met Randolph Churchill at Cowes Regatta on the Isle of Wight, an important event of the social season. Their whirlwind romance resulted in marriage in April 1874, the ceremony taking place at the British Embassy in Paris, and she took on the title Lady Randolph Churchill.

Lady Randolph was very beautiful, outgoing, and vivacious but also very intelligent and well-informed. She was, inevitably, a star of the social scene and the Churchills were poised to make a prestigious couple. Independent-minded, she always courted controversy and had a cavalier attitude to propriety. She apparently had a tattoo of a snake around her left wrist, which was most unusual for a lady of her time. She founded a short-lived literary magazine, the *Anglo-Saxon Review*. She was a firm opponent of women's suffrage (as was her son), and they drew a lot of public expressions of disapproval on this issue. She became a political figure in her own right, holding salons where prominent people of the day congregated, and she would have been an asset to her husband in his political life. Unfortunately, the marriage was not a success and from quite early on they led separate lives.

Lady Randolph's name was linked (in the euphemistic parlance of the day), with several men, including the Prince of Wales. Her patronage was valuable, as she was connected to the great and the good, and her personal charms were considerable. Her most famous affair was with the Austro-Hungarian Count Kinsky.

Winston recounts his meeting with the Count. He was invited to his aunt's London home when he was granted an exeat (permission to leave school) to attend the annual Eton versus Harrow cricket match at Lord's. He arrived to find his mother and the Count breakfasting, a situation of high impropriety. They treated him to an extraordinary and exciting day where he met

Kaiser Wilhelm, the last German Emperor, and visited the feted Crystal Palace. Churchill retained a picture of the racehorse Zoedone, which the Count had ridden to victory in the Grand National. The whole scenario was racy, but Churchill appeared quite unperturbed by the situation and was merely delighted by the interest and novelty. Sadly, this was the first time any adult had ever taken him out for enjoyment, aside from his beloved Nanny Everest.

After Randolph Churchill's early death in 1894 at the age of 45, Lady Randolph was to marry two more times. She married a Scots guardsman, George Cornwallis-West, who she divorced in 1914 after fourteen years. Then, in 1918, she married Montague Porch, an official of the Civil Service in Africa. In one of her more surprising adventures, she was found, while Churchill and his brother were both engaged in the South African War in 1900, to be acting as a volunteer nursing aide on an American hospital ship, when ladies of her station might be more usually found arranging fundraising bazaars for war efforts.

Lady Randolph's relationship with her sons was affectionate in a desultory and part-time manner. She was always far too busy. She even concealed part of their proper inheritance from them after their father's death, but this does not seem to have occasioned much resentment. It appears that Churchill's relationship with his mother was not nearly as problematic for him as that with his father. His own marriage and relationship with his children were to be very different.

# Chapter 3: Young Winston Churchill and His War Experiences

On graduation from Sandhurst, Churchill's excellent achievement and record would have afforded him a choice of suitable commissions, and it was envisioned that he might join the 60th Rifles (King's Own Rifle Corp). However, Churchill was drawn to the perceived glamour of the cavalry and joined the 4th (Queen's Own) Hussars, a regiment associated with his family over generations and favored by the social elite.

Thus, in 1895, Churchill began his military career garrisoned at Aldershot. Garrison life, however, proved very tedious to Churchill. He was determined to make his mark on the world and see some action. So, in one of his long vacation periods, he took himself off to Cuba where the Cuban War of Independence was being waged.

## Cuba, 1895

The Cuban War of Independence raged from 1895 to 1898, being the last of three wars waged by Cuban rebels against Spanish colonial rule. Churchill obtained permission to join the Spanish forces as a guest. He sailed to Havana, Cuba via New York and Florida and arrived in November 1895. He was not an actual soldier, however, and his weapons were limited to self-defense purposes.

Churchill was in Cuba for 7 weeks, during which time he saw battle and experienced being under enemy attack. He wrote in *My Early Life* that "I heard enough bullets whistle and hum past to satisfy me for some time to come". Churchill returned to the United Kingdom, and the war progressed. Toward the end of the war in 1898, the United States intervened on the side of the Cuban rebels and the war became the Spanish-American War.

Although Churchill had sympathies with the Cuban desire for self-determination and understood their criticism of inept Spanish colonial rule, he opposed the Cuban cause. He wrote in the Saturday Review in 1896 that the "...Rebel victory offers little to the world in general and Cuba in particular...Though Spanish rule is bad, Cuban government would be worse, equally corrupt, more capricious and far less stable". He can only be considered singular in deciding to spend his holidays in a war zone.

## Bangalore, India, 1896

Churchill traveled with the 4th Hussars to Bangalore in India. Even in a more exotic setting, garrison life left Churchill bored and miserable. Biographer Jacob Field recounts that he spent his time playing polo, reading, growing roses, and also making a collection of butterfly specimens that unfortunately were eaten by his terrier.

## Northwest Frontier, 1897

In July 1897, a British Army garrison situated in the Northwest Frontier Province near the border between India and Afghanistan was attacked by Pashtun tribesmen and a field force was assembled to crush the uprising. Churchill was keen to see some more action and managed to get permission to join the Bengal Lancers in the capacity of a journalist. He wrote reports for the *Daily Telegraph*, and during his time there, came under enemy fire ten times. He was mentioned in several dispatches, which were reports written by superior officers in order to immortalize brave conduct. It was during this period that he developed a taste for whiskey, which he had previously detested, as it was better than the taste of the water.

## Sudan, 1898

The Mahdist War lasted from 1881 to 1899 and was a conflict between the Anglo-Egyptian army and Sudanese Mahdists, followers of an Islamist religious teacher, Muhammed Ahmad bin Abd Allah. Originally, the fighting was between Egyptians and Sudanese Mahdists with the Egyptians being later supported by English, Belgian, and Australian forces.

In 1898, Churchill sought permission to join the 21st Bengal Lancers in Sudan. The War Office approved the transfer, but Field Marshal Lord Kitchener refused permission. It is believed Kitchener, the son of an Irish army officer, resented the entitlement of the aristocratic social elite pulling strings. Churchill returned to England in June and got his family, friends, and even the Prime Minister Lord Salisbury to intercede on his behalf. As a result, he was admitted to the Lancers in August to replace a wounded officer. Churchill would not be paid for his participation, so he arranged to work as a correspondent for the *Morning Post* to cover his expenses.

In September, Churchill had the opportunity to take part in the most significant battle of the Mahdist War, the Battle of Omdurman, which took place near Khartoum. It was to be the last cavalry charge made by the British Army. The allied forces were outnumbered but had superior weaponry and more horses. It was a horrific and bloody battle, but the Anglo-Egyptian forces triumphed. It made Kitchener a national hero in England.

On his return, Churchill wrote a commentary on the battle in which he was highly critical of Kitchener. After the battle, the enemy was either left to die or bayoneted on Kitchener's orders. Churchill considered this barbaric and inhumane. Shortly afterward, the British Army banned serving officers from acting as war correspondents; this was surely not unrelated.

Churchill was back in London in October and then rejoined his regiment in India. In 1899, he left the army and made his first foray into politics, which was always his ultimate ambition. His army career and his war writings were a place to start and to make a name for himself.

He ran in his first election in July 1899 as a Conservative Party candidate in Oldham, but he was not successful. Then, it seemed, his war zone adventures were not entirely over.

## Boer War, 1899

The Boer War was a conflict that took place in Southern Africa between Great Britain and the Orange Free State and the Transvaal (the Boer Republics). Churchill traveled there in October 1899 as a journalist for the *Morning Post*.

On November 15, 1899, the train Churchill was traveling in was ambushed by Boer forces. He was captured and taken as a prisoner of war to a camp in Pretoria. He effected a daring escape in December 1899 and stowed away on a freight train, fleeing with a bounty on his head. He was sheltered for a period by an English mine owner, hiding down in the mines and in other locations. He then escaped, again by freight train, to Portuguese East Africa (now Mozambique), hidden in a quantity of wool.

Returning to Durban, Churchill joined the South African Light Horse regiment as a lieutenant. He saw more active service participating in the Relief of Ladysmith, which was the liberation of a British garrison that had been besieged for 119 days. The soldiers suffered from extreme shortages of food and diseases, including enteric fever and typhoid. They were reduced to eating their horses and oxen, making a meat paste they called with gallows humor "chervil," mimicking the popular commercial beef extract product bovril. Churchill was also to see action at the recapture of Pretoria before returning to England in July 1900. The Boer War was to continue until 1902, changing in character to a guerilla-style conflict.

Churchill's war reporting and, most particularly, his POW escape adventure made him a celebrity. He had definitely made a name for himself and now was ready to make his definitive step into politics. However, Churchill also decided to volunteer, at the same time, for yeomanry regiments (later to be reformed into the Territorial Army), first in the Queen's Own Oxfordshire Hussars in 1900 and later in the Imperial Yeomanry in 1902 where he served as a captain. His interest in military matters and commitment to the forces always remained.

# Chapter 4: The First World War

The First World War saw Churchill grapple with the complexities of holding a political role in a military conflict. He was to employ all of his skills during this period: leadership, military intelligence and valor, effective administration, and a gift for motivating and inspiring people. As he met with success and failure, he demonstrated his resilience and versatility.

## First Lord of the Admiralty

After Churchill's exploits in the South African war, he returned to politics. He fought, won, and, very infrequently, lost seats in Oldham (later Northwest Manchester). He changed his party allegiance, joining the Liberal Party in 1904. Churchill was considered a rising political star. In 1911, he was made the First Lord of the Admiralty and still held that post at the onset of war. This position made him the political head of the Royal Navy, advisor to the government on Naval affairs, and responsible for the direction and administration of Naval Services. It was a post that had existed since the 17th century and continued until the Ministry of Defence was created to administer all services in 1964.

Churchill acquitted his duties in partnership with the First Sea Lord, Sir John Fisher, and they were an able and effective team. Churchill had anticipated the outbreak of war and had ensured the readiness of the navy as early as August 2, 1914 and had run tests of their mobilization. One of his early projects was his planned defense of Antwerp, Belgium in October 1914. Antwerp did fall, but the delay allowed for the escape of Belgian forces and effectively secured certain ports that were to be vital to the allied cause. It was simplistically seen as a failure, but there were important benefits to his action. It was a case of a battle lost that aided the winning of the war.

## A New Warfare

It quickly became evident that modern weaponry and strategy heralded a whole new kind of warfare. The First World War resulted in tragic and overwhelming loss of life. This presented a challenge not just to the military leaders and combatants but also to the political leaders who needed to build a case for war. It was also unthinkable to admit any possibility of defeat in the face of the horrific toll of casualties. This was the reality of industrial warfare.

The First World War ultimately involved thirty nations. There were 65 million volunteers who went into battle, and at the conclusion of the war, more than 16 million of them had been killed and many more were left physically or mentally damaged by the conflict. Woodrow Wilson is thought to be the first person to name the First World War "the war to end all wars," but unfortunately, it was the first major war in a century of conflict and destruction across the globe.

The roots of the war are complex but might be simplified as the prevailing belief in militarism, alliances (between European nations), imperialist ambition, and nationalist fervor. The catalyst for the war was the assassination of Archduke Franz Ferdinand, the heir to the Austro-Hungarian Empire, and his wife in Sarajevo in June 1914 by a Serbian nationalist terrorist group called the Black Hand Gang.

## Dardanelles Campaign

The Dardanelles Campaign in 1915 was one of the most controversial and devastating episodes of the First World War. Churchill was keen to open up a second front in the war as there was little progress on the Western Front. He proceeded, despite the reservation of his colleague Lord Fisher. He said in Parliament: "Are there not alternatives to sending our armies to chew barbed wire in Flanders?"

The intention was to secure the Dardanelle straits, a narrow channel connecting the Aegean Sea and the Sea of Marmara, in order to open up a route to Russia for British and allied shipping and also to oust the Ottoman Empire from the conflict. They imagined they would then be able to conquer the capital Constantinople. It would have secured the Suez Canal and British access to Middle East oil. It was also envisioned that Balkan states would then be persuaded to join the allied cause. However, they underestimated the strength and resilience of the Ottoman forces.

The allied forces were composed of a major contingent of ANZAC (Australian and New Zealand Army Corps) and other commonwealth soldiers. The campaign's Battle of Gallipoli was horrific. There were half a million casualties, with 46,000 allied dead and even more on the Ottoman side; although, they were ultimately to succeed. The forces serving in the Dardanelles suffered some of the worst of the combat environments of the First World War. There were extremes of heat and cold, causing dehydration and frostbite. They were deprived of water and food, the rations being largely inadequate and unpalatable hard biscuits and jam. They were tortured with lice, dysentery, and enteric fever resulting from the lack of sanitation. Rotting bodies piled up around them. In these conditions, they faced the full force of the Ottoman army.

The naval campaign was also under pressure from the outset and suffered great losses because of Ottoman and Turkish mines. After a naval attack failed, Admiral Robeck called off the offensive against Churchill's wishes. Robeck was supported by Prime Minister Asquith and the war administration in what was seen as a political attack on Churchill. Robeck wished to wait for infantry land-based support, which was not forthcoming until April. The intervening period allowed the Turkish forces to rally and reinforcements to reach the area. It cannot be known if keeping up the naval pressure, as Churchill advocated, would have materially altered the outcome of the campaign. What is certain is that Churchill was in the unenviable position of bearing responsibility for the campaign while not having the power to direct the action.

The failure of the Dardanelles Campaign led to Churchill losing his post, and he felt it as a bitter personal failure. Given the loss of life, a full commission of enquiry was conducted. It concluded in 1917 that he was not culpable, at least no more than any of his political colleagues.

He decided after this to leave government. He visited the frontline in France in 1915 with his yeomanry regiment, the Queen's Own Oxfordshire Hussars. Then, he obtained a commission as a lieutenant colonel in the 6th Royal Scot Fusiliers and saw active service on the Western Front. Perhaps, he saw this as a way of redeeming himself morally in the wake of Gallipoli.

When his battalion was reconfigured in 1916, he did not seek a further commission, but instead returned to the House of Commons as a private member. The coalition government appointed him in 1917 as the Minister for Munitions. This might have been seen as a lesser position than the one he held before, but it was a vital role, which Churchill threw himself into with his characteristic zeal. A minister needs to be an able administrator and manager as well as an inspiring speaker and leader, and in this role Churchill showed his versatility.

He traveled the country inspecting munitions works and interacting with the workers. One of the most important contributions was his determination to encourage the development and production of tanks. Accelerating the deployment of this new military vehicle probably sped up the conclusion of the war. In this role, he demonstrated that his determination to serve was as keen as his personal political ambition. He was to remain in this role until 1919, after the end of the war.

# Chapter 5: Churchill Between the Wars

The period between the wars was a time of mercurial fortunes for Winston Churchill.

## Parliamentary Offices, 1919-1922

Churchill was returned as a member of Parliament by his constituency of Dundee in 1918. As a member of David Lloyd George's Liberal government, he exchanged his role as the Minister for Munitions to take up the new post as the Secretary of State for Air and the Secretary of State for War. One of his first tasks was attending the Paris Peace Talks in 1919. He was not personally responsible for the brokering of peace but participated in discussions envisioning the new face of Europe following the trauma of the First World War.

## Churchill and the Middle East

In 1921, Churchill became the Secretary of State for the Colonies, and organized the Cairo Conference concerning Iraq and the Middle East. The conference was an innovative meeting, designed to minimize bureaucracy and maximize pragmatism. Churchill convened military and civilian leaders and was guided by his friend T.E Lawrence (Lawrence of Arabia). Costly British land forces were withdrawn and replaced with a military air presence. Decisions were made concerning the government of Transjordan, Iraq, Lebanon, and Syria. There were pre-existing and contradictory agreements with both the Arabs and the Jews concerning Palestine. Discussions with these parties were to result in a white paper presented the following year that designated Palestine as a Jewish homeland but instated continuing rights to Arabs.

## Personal Losses, 1921

1921 was a year of personal losses for Churchill. His mother died. Shortly thereafter he and his wife, Clementine, endured the tragic death of their daughter, Marigold. He continued to apply himself to his work with characteristic stoicism and emotional control.

## The Irish Question, 1921

The political situation in Ireland where the Irish War of Independence was being fought in 1921 was never Churchill's responsibility, but he was strenuous in his support for a continuance of British rule as the Irish treaty of 1921 was negotiated and Ireland was partitioned. He had argued, however, for Ireland to remain united and be given a degree of self-governance.

## Chanak Crisis, 1922

The threat of war arose against Turkey, which was in conflict with Greece regarding territories adjacent to the Dardanelles in what was called the Chanak Crisis. There was a small British military presence there that was felt to be under threat. The majority of the government was reluctant to engage. Churchill backed Lloyd George, his leader and friend, in pressing for a British intervention. In the end, without foreign intervention, the Turks were victorious and a settlement was made granting Greece the territories they wanted while securing Constantinople for the Turks. This episode was seen as a lack of judgment on the part of Lloyd George that undermined his authority and the fortunes of the Liberal Party. A weakened Liberal Party sought a pact with Ramsey McDonald's Labour Party in order to defeat the Conservatives. Churchill, a committed anti-socialist and anti-Bolshevik, resigned, as he could not support such an alliance.

Churchill failed to retain his Dundee seat in the 1922 election, as he was suffering from acute appendicitis and was unable to campaign. He was to ruefully recall in an article "Election Memories" published in the *Strand Magazine* in 1931 that "In the twinkling of an eye I found myself without an office, without a seat, without party and without an appendix".

He did, however, manage to find and buy his home Chartwell in Essex, which he loved deeply. He was to reside there until just before his death.

1923 and 1924 were to see him lose two further elections where he stood as an independent (anti-socialist) constitutionalist: an election in West Leicester and a by-election for Westminster Abbey. Before the year was out, though, he had secured the constituency of Epping, which he was to hold for decades. By December, he had been approached by Stanley Baldwin, leader of the Conservatives newly in power, to hold the very senior office of Chancellor of the Exchequer (equivalent to the treasury secretary in the United States). Churchill was again crossing the floor and rejoining the Conservative Party he had left in 1904.

## Chancellor of the Exchequer, 1924-1929

Churchill presented five budgets to the house during his tenure as Chancellor of the Exchequer. Being offered the post was a surprise, not in the least to himself. Churchill was an economic liberal, an anti-protectionist, and an advocate of free trade ideals. He was regarded by his colleagues with some suspicion and mistrust, but Stanley Baldwin must have considered him a "safe pair of hands" as Britain struggled to recover economically and emotionally from the First World War.

## Gold Standard

Churchill's first major decision as Chancellor of the Exchequer was to restore the gold standard. This strengthened the British pound and brought it into closer alignment with the U.S. dollar. It did, however, put pressure on British exports and industry profits, particularly those of the mining industry. It was generally regarded as a prudent move at the time. Churchill said, "It will shackle us to reality." He was later to regard it as a major mistake and personal failure because of its contribution to the slide into global depression.

## The General Strike, 1926

The falling profits of the mining industry resulted in a catastrophic decline in miner's wages. At the time, the trade unions in Britain were extremely powerful. Industrial action by the National Union of Mineworkers was supported by other members of the Trade Unions Council, resulting in a nationwide stoppage by 1.7 million workers with transport and heavy industry workers coming out for the miners. It lasted for nine days in May 1926.

Churchill supported the government, which refused to bow to this pressure to intervene between the mine owners and mine workers. The armed services and middle- and upper-class volunteers took over essential services, driving buses and delivering food and milk.

When the printworkers stopped working, effectively silencing the press, Churchill acted as an editor of the British Gazette that was produced and distributed by volunteers. He is quoted in the Gazette, saying, "I decline utterly to be impartial, as between fire brigade and fire".

The left-wing press cast him as a villain, oblivious to the plight of mine workers, who had seen a weekly wage drop from £6 to £3.90 a week. In fact, Churchill had spoken in the House, advocating the setting of a minimum wage for miners and a restriction on the profits to be drawn by owners. Stanley Baldwin had awarded a temporary subsidy to the miners to augment wages, which Churchill had opposed, believing it was supporting a failing and mismanaged industry. He said the subsidy was awarded "over my blood-stained corpse." The effect of the General Strike was to intensify and accelerate the decline of the mining industry, despite the justness of the miners' cause. Resultingly, Churchill is a figure of hatred in many former mining areas in Britain to this day.

In 1927, Churchill met Mussolini, the Prime Minister of Italy, and spoke well of him as he saw him as a deterrent to communism and admired his economic and fiscal prudence. He did not equate Italian Fascism with German Nazism. To him, it was communism and Nazism that were the "Infernal Twins" or "Creeds of the Devil that menaced Europe". In 1928, he imposed the first petrol (or gas) tax in Britain as part of his fourth budget. His fifth budget in 1929 was to be his last. He retained his Epping seat in the elections, but the Conservatives lost office and Churchill lost his cabinet post. He also lost a personal fortune in the Wall Street Crash of 1929.

## Wilderness Years

1929 was the start of the most depressing and unhappy decade of Churchill's life. He was to refer to the years from 1929 to 1939 as his "years in the wilderness." He was frustrated politically at this time, often a lone voice in the House of Commons. He was outspoken with views that were not widely held, and he was seen as a maverick. During this time, he also suffered from his first depressive episodes, which he termed his "Black Dogs."

However, he remained characteristically active and productive beyond the power of most mortals. He traveled extensively, including to Canada and the United States, where he met President Herbert Hoover at the White House. He also traveled on the continent of Europe. He published a number of books, including the autobiographical *My Early Life* in 1930, as well as newspaper and magazine articles.

# Churchill and India

Churchill took a resolute stand against Indian calls for independence as claimed by the Indian National Congress (INC), spearheaded by Mahatma Gandhi. They wanted independence of at least dominion status. Predominantly white colonies, like Canada and Australia (indigenous people being largely ignored), were dominions, and even Egypt and Iraq had a degree of self-rule.

Detractors claimed Churchill's opposition was a cynical ploy to bolster his failing political career by invoking the British Empire and appealing to nationalist sentiment. Churchill declared a belief that British rule was better for India. He felt that the religious and caste divisions in Indian society would lead to increasing inequality and rifts and result in bloodshed. Indian independence did lead to bloody civil war and the partition of India ultimately, but it is questionable whether that gave Britain the right to deny India self-determination.

Churchill was perceived by many as rude and racist in his response to Gandhi, describing him as a "seditious Middle Temple lawyer, now posing as a fakir of a type well known in the East striding half-naked up the steps of the viceregal palace, while he is organizing and conducting a campaign of civil disobedience".

He resigned from the shadow cabinet over this issue and found himself even more politically marginalized; although, he continued to be a compelling, if controversial voice, from the backbenches.

## The Abdication

Churchill also alienated himself by supporting King Edward VIII in the constitutional crisis provoked by King Edward VIII's desire to marry the American divorcée Wallis Simpson. It was not permissible for him to marry a divorced person. Churchill argued for a morganatic marriage, which would allow King Edward VIII to marry, with his wife and children remaining commoners, rather than holding the titles of Queen, Princes, or Princesses. This solution was not accepted by the government. Churchill assumed that King Edward VIII would then bow to the inevitable and end the relationship, not thinking he would ever step down from the throne. He was very sympathetic to King Edward VIII, who was a personal friend (Churchill had met him during his time as the First Lord of the Admiralty and when King Edward VIII had been a naval cadet). To Churchill, abdication was a dereliction of royal duty, and he was disappointed.

# Rearmament and Appeasement

The most important political stance Churchill took during his wilderness years was his persistent and strenuous warnings regarding rearmament in Germany and the relative British unpreparedness for war. The government was struggling against a worldwide depression and there was no public or political taste for spending on the military and arms. Churchill continually reported on the levels of tanks and planes being produced in Germany, to groans and boos of derision.

He was also deeply alarmed by the Nazi ideology and the growing level of support for Adolf Hitler in Germany. German diplomats protested against Churchill's outspoken statements about potential German aggression. His political colleagues believed the country wanted peace at all costs.

Prime Minister Neville Chamberlain believed in a policy of appeasement, making concessions to Hitler and thereby building a relationship with him with a view to avoid war. He thought Hitler could, in this way, be contained and restrained, but he was wrong. Since 1935, German rearmament had continued apace; in 1936, German troops were moved into the Rhineland (an area close to the borders with France, Belgium, Luxembourg, and the Netherlands). These actions were in clear contravention of the Treaty of Versailles signed after the First World War, and Hitler was violating this without any action being taken.

The now notorious Munich Agreement of 1938 had France, the United Kingdom, and Nazi Germany signing a pact under which Germany was given the rights to occupy the Sudeten area on the German-Czechoslovakian border. Prime Minister Neville Chamberlain returned after the meetings and said, "I believe it is peace for our time." Days later, Churchill was to say in a broadcast to the United States that "the lights are going out; but there is still time for those to whom freedom and parliamentary government mean something, to consult together".

Though branded a warmonger by opponents, Churchill continued to criticize his government. He felt Britain had abandoned a defenseless Czechoslovakia and was proved right when Hitler proceeded to invade the entire country. His assessment of a policy of appeasement was that it was a tacit acknowledgement that the appeaser was not strong enough to defy an aggressor and that concessions avoided a war but weakened the appeaser and strengthened the opponent. He said: "An appeaser is one who feeds a crocodile, hoping it will eat him last".

Hitler's defiance and militarism continued and increased. It was clear that Churchill had been right all along. The invasion of Poland by Hitler and the Nazi forces on September 1, 1939, was the precipitating action. By September 3rd, Britain and France declared war on Germany. The Soviet Union joined the allies on September 17th.

The Second World War had begun.

# Chapter 6: The Second World War

Churchill described 1940 as Britain's "finest hour." The Second World War and 1940, in particular, is undoubtedly Churchill's finest hour, too. He was keenly aware that he was meeting his destiny and taking on the greatest role and responsibility of his life.

## First Lord of the Admiralty, 1939-1940

Churchill was returned to the post of the First Lord of the Admiralty, which he had held during the First World War. There is a, perhaps apocryphal, story that the navy wired the message, "Winston is back!" He was incredibly happy to be back in office with an important role to fulfill. He was determined to establish a good working relationship with his First Sea Lord and Chief of the Naval Staff. His tireless work, endless demands for detailed reports, and exhortations for his staff to press on motivated and galvanized his team.

Churchill was in a key role at this early stage of the war, called in Britain the "Phoney War" as not a lot seemed to be happening to the people of Britain. What was going on was sea-based initiatives. The naval fleet faced the challenge of extensive

German sea mining and U-boats (*unterseeboots*), the German craft capable of undersea and surface attacks.

The most significant early victory was the capture of the Admiral Graf Spee, a German pocket battleship, during the Battle of the River Plate near Montevideo in Uruguay. Then, attention was given to securing Norwegian waters, but in this objective, the British failed. Norway was ultimately occupied by the Germans.

The failure of the Norwegian campaign led to debates in the British Parliament, which were damaging to the government. On May 10, 1940, Germany invaded France, Belgium, Luxembourg, and the Netherlands. Engagement with British and French troops signaled that the Phoney War was over. Prime Minister Neville Chamberlain resigned, and there was a decision to form a coalition government of national unity to fight the war. Churchill was chosen to lead the new government. On the evening of May 10th, he went to Buckingham Palace to see King George VI, and became the Prime Minister.

## Prime Minister, 1940-1945

Churchill was very moved by his appointment at his country's hour of greatest need. He said he felt "that all my past life had been but a preparation for this hour and for this trial." There was strong approval for his appointment. The Labour politician

Hugh Dalton acknowledged he was "the only man we have for this hour."

Churchill assembled a cabinet from across the political spectrum. He included former premier Neville Chamberlain and Labour leader Clement Atlee. Anthony Eden (who had been a prominent anti-appeasement voice) soon succeeded Lord Halifax as the Secretary of State for Foreign, Commonwealth, and Development Affairs. Ernest Bevan joined later as the Minister for Labour and National Service. Lord Beaverbrook, Churchill's friend, was to hold various posts during the war, serving as the Minister for Aircraft Production, the Minister of Supply, and the Minister of War Production.

Churchill also sought the advice of civilian advisers, including the scientist Professor Frederick Lindemann. Although brilliant, Lindemann was abrasive, arrogant and stubborn, so his appointment was unpopular. It was a Churchillian innovation to include technocrats and experts in industry and other disciplines directly in government. He brought in the German refugee scientists who were to warn of the development of nuclear capability in Germany and lend their knowledge to what became the Manhattan Project, which was responsible for producing the first nuclear weapons. Brilliant mathematical minds, such as Alan Turing's, were put to work in code-breaking at Bletchley Park.

Churchill made himself the Minister of Defense, giving himself oversight and full control of all the services, not wishing to find himself, as he had been in the First War, held responsible although unable to direct actions.

After appointing his cabinet, Churchill addressed the House of Commons in the brief but historic speech in which he told them he "had nothing to offer but blood, toil, sweat and tears" as they faced an "ordeal of the most grievous kind," with the aim of "victory at all costs." He then departed for France where the threat of invasion was imminent.

## Dunkirk, 1940

Fighting in Northern France, during the Battle of France, left the French forces and the British Expeditionary Force troops who had gone to assist them surrounded by Germans on the Normandy coast. They had suffered heavy casualties and lost a great deal of equipment. Between May 26th and June 4th, the daring Operation Dynamo evacuated French and British troops from the beaches at Dunkirk. Naval vessels were joined by civilian ships and a flotilla of small craft, pleasure boats, and lifeboats, which participated to ferry the trapped servicemen to larger ships for evacuation. It was a brave and highly successful exercise. As Churchill reminded people, an evacuation was not a victory, but 338,226 men were brought to safety with the aid of 800 vessels.

# Fall of Paris, 1940

The fall of Paris and occupation of France began on June 14, 1940. Churchill had argued for France not to surrender, but in the absence of U.S. support, the French conceded. They signed an armistice and a puppet government under Marshal Pétain was moved south from Paris to Vichy, the unoccupied zone of the French mainland.

# Cabinet War Crisis, 1940

Following the fall of France and the evacuation at Dunkirk, Lord Halifax and others contended that Britain, too, should pursue peace with Hitler and try to make terms and end the war. Churchill was utterly determined that it was essential to the survival of the free world that Britain fight on. He managed to carry the cabinet and the House of Commons with him, using the full power of his rhetoric.

# Battle of Britain, 1940

When the Battle of France had been lost, Churchill announced the onset of the Battle of Britain. It was now inevitable that Germany would try to invade the mainland of Britain. Hitler planned an invasion he had named Operation Sealion, which depended on first disabling Britain's air defenses.

Between July and October 1940, the Royal Air Force (RAF) and the Fleet Air Arm (FAA) of the Royal Navy mounted a mighty campaign. Fighter Command of the RAF, flying in the famous Hurricanes and Spitfires airplanes, attacked German industry and ports. RAF pilots included men from all over the world. There were entire battalions of Polish and Czech pilots.

Coastal command carried out intelligence gathering flights, patrolled to identify attacks, and bombed shipping and industrial sites, too. They were supported by a vast ground crew of engineers and WAAFs (Women's Auxiliary Air Force), women who were radar operators and plotters in the command centers. Barrage balloons over cities helped to mitigate air attack and anti-aircraft platforms were built out in the sea of the Thames Estuary.

The German offensives, at first, concentrated on airfields and air command centers, then moved to a concentrated campaign of bombing London in September 1940. The extraordinary bravery and considerable sacrifice of the RAF meant that by September 15th, the Luftwaffe had been repelled to the extent that the German Operation Sealion invasion could no longer occur.

Churchill was to make a famous speech in August 1940, stating that "Never in the field of human conflict has so much been owed by so many to so few." Britain had gone to war ill-equipped. In the absence of anything else, Churchill's stirring speeches became a weapon. Journalist Beverley Nichols said Churchill "took the English language and sent it into battle."

## The Blitz, 1940-1941

The Blitz was the name given to the sustained campaign of bombing waged by the Luftwaffe from September 1940 to May 1941. It targeted British cities, mainly London, and the aim was to destroy industry and the docks. At one point, London was bombed every day and night for nearly three months. A third of London was destroyed, especially the East End. When Buckingham Palace was hit, Queen Mary said, "Now I can look East London in the eye."

When sirens sounded, Londoners took refuge in underground stations. Early in the war, Churchill had the Cabinet War Rooms constructed beneath the Treasury in Whitehall. When his official London residence, 10 Downing Street, was bombed, he declined to move out of London. He spent his time in the Cabinet War Rooms, like Londoners, taking refuge underground.

Churchill had a vital role in bolstering the morale of the British people in the face of such prolonged and fearful suffering. He traveled tirelessly to the places that had been bombed and spoke with the people affected. He demonstrated the famous "Blitz Spirit" of defiance, stoicism, and humor in the face of loss.

After raids, business premises that had been bombed and partly destroyed posted signs saying "More open than usual" and the people "kept calm and carried on." Churchill was to recall in his World War Two memoirs that Londoners were "seen at their best...grim and dirty, dogged and serviceable, with the confidence of an unconquered people in their bones, they adapted themselves to this strange new life of the Blitz, with all its terrors, with all its jolts and jars."

Churchill also traveled abroad frequently during the war, visiting troops and combat zones, and also attending conferences and holding meetings with allied leaders. He was 65 years old when the war began, but colleagues remarked he appeared younger, so animated and motivated he was by the greatest challenge of his life. He was quite capable of regularly working eighteen-hour days, which was difficult for many staff, even those much younger than him. He could be challenging to work with, sometimes rude and demanding, but as Field Marshall Brooke remarked, "It is worth all these difficulties to have the privilege of working with such a man."

Churchill could, equally, be very charming. It was during this period that his wife had to intervene and tell him he was "rough, sarcastic, and overbearing" to his colleagues. He was not invincible, though. In 1941, while visiting the White House, he suffered a heart attack (although, he defied the doctor's orders for bed rest), and in 1943, he contracted severe pneumonia.

# Pearl Harbor, 1941

The Japanese attack on the U.S. naval base Pearl Harbor in Hawaii lasted a little more than an hour but resulted in over 2,000 casualties and 18 lost or damaged ships. The Japanese intention was to wipe out the United States' capacity to obstruct them in their campaign to occupy South East Asia. The impact of Pearl Harbor was immense.

Domestically, U.S. civilians of German, Italian, Japanese, or Italian descent were interned in camps within the United States. The United States then entered World War Two. Until then, it had maintained a neutral stance, supplying the allies with food and goods.

# Battle of the Atlantic, 1939-1945

The Battle of the Atlantic, which included defending and maintaining the transport of food and supplies to Britain and Allied Europe, was a campaign that continued throughout the Second World War. It was central to all aspects of the war. Churchill confessed in his memoir that the only thing that truly scared him in the war was "the U-boat peril."

# Fall of Singapore, 1942

In his memoir of the Second World War, Churchill described the Japanese invasion and consequent Fall of Singapore as the worst defeat in British military history. Some historians blame Churchill for not honoring promises to adequately defend Malaysia, with the naval fleet heavily engaged in the Battle of the Atlantic and airpower focused on attacking Germany.

The fate of Allied Forces in the face of Japanese victories and the Japanese inhuman treatment of prisoners of war, even women and children, was horrific. Burma was part of the British Empire in the Second World War. When it was captured by Japan in 1942, troops struggled to regain it. The Burma Road was the only supply route open to China, but the coastline was blocked by the Japanese.

British Forces, with many troops from India and Africa, and Nepalese Gurkhas fought under the harshest conditions until 1945. Then, a retreat was decided, but the retreat was the longest in military history: 1,000 miles on foot to the Indian border in unspeakable conditions.

Churchill was focused on the European arena of war. He also knew Britain could not hope to challenge Japan without U.S. support. He claimed he was unaware of the lack of defenses in the region: "I ought to have known and I ought to have asked [but] the possibility of Singapore having no land-ward defences no more entered into my mind than that of a battleship being launched without a bottom."

## El Alamein, 1942

The Battle of El Alamein was a decisive victory at the end of the campaign in North Africa. The German and Italians under Rommel were defeated by Field Marshal Montgomery and General Alexander. Allied troops had an advantage of superior arms and equipment. It secured the region until the United States and other Allied troops, landing in Morocco in 1943, ended the campaign. It was a key turning point in the war in favor of the Allies.

Churchill had been dismayed by the fortunes of the Eighth Army campaign and traveling to the region, in his typical hands-on fashion, had determined that a change in leadership was required, and he was instrumental in Montgomery and Alexander being deployed to the region. Churchill acknowledged the victory but warned it was "not the end, not even the beginning of the end, but possibly the end of the beginning."

# The Battle of Stalingrad, 1943

The Battle of Stalingrad was a huge victory for the Allies in Russia. As Churchill said, the war here "tore the guts out of the German war machine." After the Battle of Stalingrad in February 1943, Hitler had no possibility of succeeding on the Eastern Front and his eventual defeat was inevitable. But this came at an extraordinary human cost. One million Soviets were killed at Stalingrad alone. Geoffrey Roberts believes the contribution of the Soviets to the Second World War was "rewritten during the Cold War" and the world outside Russia barely acknowledged the 60th year anniversary (in 2003) of what was probably the most decisive turning point of the Second World War.

# Holocaust

Churchill was aware of the persecution of the Jewish people in Germany in the prelude to war and spoke out against it. He received intelligence reports of ongoing persecutions and transportation. In 1941, following deportations from Paris, he said in a broadcast, "None has suffered more cruelly than the Jew the unspeakable evils wrought upon the bodies and spirits of men by Hitler and his vile regime...He has borne and continues to bear a burden that might have seemed beyond endurance...Assuredly in the day of victory the Jew's suffering and his part in this struggle will not be forgotten."

When the end of the war and the liberation of concentration camps by allied forces revealed the full extent of the atrocities, Churchill's response was to condemn "the most horrible crime ever committed in the whole history of the world." He called for "all concerned in this crime...including those only obeyed orders by carrying out these butcheries, should be put to death after their association with the murders has been proved."

## Surrender

April 1945 saw the accelerating surrender of German forces across Europe. The Allies took millions of prisoners. The Germans left Finland. Mussolini was killed by Italian resistance forces. Hitler committed suicide. Soviet, American, and British forces liberated the concentration camps; weakened prisoners, sadly, continued to die and others became part of a great wave of displaced people and refugees.

## VE Day, 1945

Churchill addressed jubilant crowds in London on VE (Victory in Europe) Day on May 8, 1945. He spoke of a British victory: "We were the first, in this ancient island, to draw the sword against tyranny...against the most tremendous military power that has been seen. We were alone for a whole year."

## Post-War Statesman

After the war, Churchill's Conservative government was defeated, and he found himself out of office. He traveled and gave talks in the United States, including a famous address at a college in Missouri in 1946 when he spoke about an "Iron Curtain" having descended across the continent of Europe. The Cold War, dividing East and West for more than forty years, had begun.

His political interest in these years centered on the importance of building strong international alliances for Britain. He wanted a special relationship between the United States and Britain, as well as alliances with Europe that were political and economic. He believed this three-way alliance structure would secure and maintain peace. He also wanted to preserve the ties with the empire and commonwealth: "With deep grief, I watch the clattering down of the British Empire with all its glories and all the services it has rendered to mankind," he said, ever the imperialist in the face of a very different world.

He served again as the Prime Minister when the Conservatives returned to power in 1951 and stayed in the role until 1955, very much the elder statesman. He was determined to be a steadying force as Britain rebuilt after the war, but he was a Prime Minister made for war, not peacetime. He suffered a serious stroke in 1953 and was to retire from the cabinet in 1955. He remained an MP representing Woodford until the year before his death in 1965. He had been a member of Parliament continuously from 1900 until 1964, with only one short break between 1922 and 1924.

# Chapter 7: Churchill's Personal Life

An examination of Churchill's personal life offers insight into the strengths and contradictions of the man. He was, in many ways, the product of his background: upper class, privileged, conservative, and rooted in the Victorian era in which he was born. He was also something of an eccentric figure with a personality that was endearing and exasperating in equal measure.

## Clementine Churchill

Churchill married Clementine Hozier in 1908. She was the main emotional and practical pillar of support in his life, and they enjoyed a close and affectionate, if at times turbulent, union for over 57 years.

They first met at a ball where Clementine found him shy and awkward, and then they met again later at a dinner party where they sat together and spoke. Churchill was deeply impressed by this intelligent and engaging woman. She was ten years his junior and a striking, if not startlingly beautiful, woman. He proposed to her in the Temple of Diana summerhouse on the grounds of Blenheim Palace. They married at St. Margaret's, Westminster after a 5-month courtship with frequent meetings and a lively correspondence.

Clementine was the daughter of Sir Henry Hozier, a Scottish aristocrat, and his wife, Blanche. She had an extraordinary and challenging childhood. Her parents had a tempestuous marriage, and her mother engaged in a number of well-publicized affairs. There was always speculation as to her true biological parentage.

When her parents finally separated, her mother, who was a great gambler, was left without means. She and her children lived a peripatetic and uncertain life. This left Clementine with a lifelong fear of poverty. She also, however, grew up to be resourceful, independent, and capable of earning her own living, which was unusual for the daughter of an aristocrat at the turn of the century.

As a wife, Clementine was unfailingly loyal and supportive of her husband, not just at home, but in his career. She had a keen interest and involvement in politics in her own right, not always agreeing with Churchill. He relied on her judgment and intelligent criticism. In the wars, she set to work on her own projects, which included establishing canteens in munitions factories in the First World War and working with the Red Cross and in support of Russian refugees in the Second.

Clementine joined the Liberal Party when Churchill did but remained a Liberal all her life, even when Churchill rejoined the Conservative Party. In fact, while he was a Conservative

Minister, she held meetings of the local Liberal Party in their home, Chartwell in Essex. They also clashed over women's suffrage with Churchill being against votes for women and her in favor. However, Clementine was to intervene physically to pull him to safety by his coattails when a suffragette tried to push him under a train shortly after their marriage. After Churchill's death, she was made a Baroness and sat in the House of Lords in her own right as a cross-bencher; although, her career there was curtailed by deafness.

Life with Churchill could be challenging, given his mercurial temperament, episodes of depression (his famous Black Dogs), and his tireless and uncompromising work ethic. Clementine was also disturbed by his reckless financial extravagance, which triggered the insecurities of her childhood. She was known to take the occasional break, traveling alone to escape the tension.

There is the suggestion that during an extended trip to Borneo, Celebes (now Sulawesi), and other South Sea Islands, she had a dalliance, if not an actual affair, with a charming young art dealer, Terence Phillips, which Churchill jealousy suspected.

But Churchill is believed to have had an affair with Doris Castlerosse, who was a glamorous socialite and one of the aristocratic hostesses he stayed with when visiting the South of France. He ended the affair as the approaching Second World War claimed his attention. Later in the war, she attempted to blackmail him, armed with a painting he made of her, which she believed would confirm their affair. He helped her escape back to Britain when travel was difficult to arrange. Lord Beaverbrook, his political colleague but also a press baron (otherwise known as a newspaper publisher), was able to retrieve the painting and hush up the scandal that might have damaged him politically.

When Clementine heard of the affair later, she was saddened, but it did not threaten their marriage.

Clementine's loyalty was unflinching and shown in different ways. When Churchill was insulted at a dinner she attended while traveling, she left and when an apology was not forthcoming the next day, traveled home. When he died, Clementine destroyed a painting made of him by Graham Sutherland, which he hated, even though it was valuable and she personally admired it.

Clementine was ever his sagacious, devoted, and beloved Clem Cat.

## Children

Churchill and Clementine had five children. His relationship with them was very different from his own unhappy experience. He was very affectionate, devoted, and prone to spoiling them. However, both he and Clementine were always extremely busy with their own lives. Tragedy struck in 1921 when their daughter,

Marigold, died from septicemia. They were devastated, but in their fashion, bore it stoically.

A daughter, Mary, was born soon after, and they were very much closer to this daughter, perhaps clinging to her in their loss. Mary worked closely with her father, especially during the war. Randolph, the only son, followed his father into politics but was always, understandably, in his father's shadow. He suffered from serious and suicidal depression. Sarah, who became an actress and dancer, had multiple and very troubled relationships. Diana, their eldest child, ended her life by suicide.

## Animals

Animals were very important to Churchill. The most famous pet is probably his bulldog, Dodo, yet there were also two brown poodles who were both named Rufus (Rufus 1 and Rufus 2). One can only imagine that Jock, the marmalade cat, and Nelson, who was the cat who assisted Churchill during the war, ruled Churchill in the feline fashion and steered the course of history. Chartwell was home to all sorts of animals, including swans, ducks, pigs, and goats, and Churchill loved to see them. He used animal analogies in his talks and writings. Political appeasers were "people who fed crocodiles," and he spoke of a friend as having "all the canine qualities" (this was a compliment).

Of course, a love of horses remained with him throughout his life from his early years with warhorses as a cavalry officer to polo ponies and later racehorses. The goldfish that appear in some of his paintings of Chartwell were, in fact, not goldfish but golden orfe that required a special sort of high protein mealworm type food. There is a bizarre story where Churchill prevailed upon the Australian embassy to send him a number of platypuses (this being during the war when you might have imagined him to be engaged with other matters). Unfortunately, they perished en route. The delightful intention was to establish a platypussery at the London Zoo where citizens would send earthworms in jars of soil for their nourishment.

## Dress

Churchill was inclined toward a formal and gentlemanly style of dressing, inspired by his Edwardian youth with morning coats and bow ties. He was outfitted by the Savile Row tailors, Henry Poole. Apparently, the craftsmen were delighted by his sense of style but in later years faced the challenge of cutting the clothes to flatter his fuller figure.

In his youth, he had been a striking figure in a cavalry uniform. He is famous for an eccentric outfit he called a siren suit, which is an all-in-one garment rather like a jumpsuit but looser and with long sleeves. He had many of these made by the shirtmakers Turnbull and Asser of Jermyn Street in a variety of fabrics from green velvet to chalk-stripe cashmere twill. They were probably comfortable and practical, but certainly unusual.

He sported a homburg hat or a bowler hat, the former perhaps in imitation of the highly stylish Foreign Secretary Anthony Eden. Since the popularity of a recent film about Churchill, *Darkest Hour* (2017), the same tailors and hatters have made available copies of Churchillian garments. Apparently, it is possible to purchase a replica of the peculiar beige, fuzzy teddy bear overcoat in which he appears in various photographs for around £2000, as well as siren suits.

## Painting

Painting was a lifelong hobby and source of relaxation for Churchill. He traveled with paints and easels and created over 500 paintings in his lifetime. He admired and was influenced by the impressionists and post-impressionists, particularly Paul Cézanne. In his many visits to the South of France, which he loved, he endeavored to paint in the same fabled light.

He was an extremely accomplished, if not a great painter. Others wanted him to submit his paintings to the Royal Academy, which he only agreed to do under a pseudonym. He was exhibited and thus became an "RA," the establishment hallmark of a good painter. Painting remained a refuge, and he documented his travels, his homes, and the places he loved and shared with friends and family. His work always commanded good prices and Churchill made gifts of paintings to staff he appreciated.

## Bricklaying

Another eccentric hobby was Churchill's enthusiasm for bricklaying. He was proficient and productive enough to earn a bricklayers union card and would frequently record in his diary "laid 200 bricks today." One can only imagine he enjoyed pride in perfecting a practical skill and found the repetitive nature of the activity meditative and soothing.

## Life at Chartwell

Former employees attest to a life at Chartwell that was very eventful and exciting. They were challenged to work hard but the atmosphere was supportive, friendly, and inclusive. His long-suffering secretaries found themselves often working until two in the morning, but despite his tempers, outbursts, and strange habits, they all adored him. Secretary Nonie Chapman recalled being sent to the station to pick up food for the golden orfe fish and also the films to be shown in Chartwell's private cinema to which everyone was invited, staff and family.

Dr. Maurice Ashley, as a young research assistant in the 1930s, found himself challenged by being served with quantities of alcohol to which he was not accustomed. When he tried to decline port, Churchill, concerned about being a good host, immediately arranged for Madeira wine to be substituted, to the young man's dismay. Mention is often made of the large quantities of alcohol Churchill consumed, starting in the morning, with daily pints of champagne, beer, port, and lots of whiskey and water (the whiskey and water being extremely weak mixtures). By any standards, this consumption is very high, but he never appeared inebriated, and if he was drinking at an alcoholic level, it did not seem to impede his abilities.

There were many instances when Churchill showed great generosity and kindness to his staff. Apart from gifts, when the wife of his chauffeur fell ill, he required the whole family to drive themselves in the evenings so the man could be at home. He was also very tolerant, as long as people seemed to be trying.

Chartwell was a lively environment. Churchill chose eccentric and exciting friends. Lawrence of Arabia was a frequent visitor, and the visitors' book is signed by film stars like Charlie Chaplin and Vivien Leigh.

Running a place like Chartwell was very expensive. The lavish lifestyle strained the family finances; neither Churchill nor Clementine inherited any fortune. As has been mentioned, this troubled Clementine. Churchill considered it a point of pride that by his own work, more by writing than politics, he was able to maintain the lifestyle of an aristocratic gentleman, traveling and entertaining as well as educating his children privately.

# Chapter 8: Churchill, the Writer and the Politician

Churchill was a man with an extraordinary breadth of talents. He was a consummate politician, but his career as a writer was as distinguished, successful, and more lucrative, if not so widely known.

## Politician

Churchill was born to be a politician. It would seem to have been his ambition in life all along, and the military career of his youth was more of a starter career and a way to make his name and gain worldly experience before he entered politics. Churchill started his political career as might be expected for someone of his class, background, and heritage as a Conservative.

However, joining the Liberals was an unexpected move. He quarreled with his party over protectionism and trade tariffs. Changing political parties was termed "ratting" in Parliament and the "rat" was liable to be a figure of distrust. The Liberal Party's economic beliefs were similar to his own. He was always a classic liberal in his economic views and committed to free trade. He rose in power quickly in this party, becoming the Secretary of State for the Home Department and then the First

Lord of the Admiralty at an astonishingly young age. He found on the Liberal benches a great friend in David Lloyd George, and the men were to remain lifelong friends, party allegiances notwithstanding.

In his defection to the Liberals, he was accused of being opportunistic and seeking power for selfish reasons, when in fact he was directed by his strongly held beliefs and principles. He was a political animal of acute and incisive judgment on many matters of state, much more than being a party animal. He believed in loyalty to colleagues and friends, but that loyalty was not strong enough to sway him against his principles or what he saw as the best interest of his country.

Churchill was to recross the floor again in 1925 when the Conservative Prime Minister offered him the very senior post of Chancellor of the Exchequer, considered second only to the Premiership. It would give Churchill a position of real power and the opportunity to have the greatest possible influence on national (and international) affairs.

Churchill was never afraid to court controversy and stand alone on an issue. Most famously of all was his dogged insistence that Britain needed to rearm in the face of German rearmament in the 1930s, and that Hitler needed to be challenged as a tyrant, dictator, and aggressor rather than appeased as his government intended. He took the world to war against Nazism, always believing that earlier action against Hitler could have prevented the war.

Probably, Churchill was equally suited to the Conservative Party. Many of his attitudes reflected his Victorian and Edwardian upbringing and upper-class origins. His opposition to women's suffrage was difficult to comprehend as he was the son and the spouse of intelligent, politically astute, and assertive women whose opinions he valued; however, it was a classically conservative stance.

Churchill was an imperialist, believing in the superiority of British rule and civilization. His views on Indian independence were extremely right wing and show him in a bad light. He was keen for India to remain part of the British Empire, even though it was clearly disintegrating around him. He felt India was better off under British rule but acted to protect the rights of British cotton importers to the detriment of Indian producers.

His views on Ireland were complex, and he always supported home rule and a degree of self-determination for Ireland but thought British rule should ultimately remain. He opposed the partition of Ireland in 1921. One of his most criticized actions was to support the deployment of the violent and renegade Black and Tan troops to assist the Irish Constabulary in suppressing the IRA.

On the contrary, his views on economics and welfare rights and reforms were liberal and progressive. He was at home on both sides of the house, and at his best in the coalition national government of the war, with the best minds from either end of the spectrum uniting to solve the task at hand.

Churchill was a man focused on issues, whether his judgment was defensible or not. He did not build political support around himself and strategize his career and rise to power by subterfuge or Machiavellian networking. When he built his own cabinet, he invited the best minds and administrators, whatever their political colors. He also included friends, but only when they had specific and useful expertise, as in the case of Lord Beaverbrook who, as a newspaper mogul, had influence and understood world affairs, communications, and media.

## Man of Words

The world is so enthralled by the image of Churchill as a great leader and statesman that there is a tendency to overlook his parallel career and the extraordinary gift that was instrumental to his political achievement. He was a magician with words, written or verbal, and his output was prodigious. Churchill published many books, including memoirs, an autobiography called *My Early Life,* biographies of his father and of his 17th-century ancestor the First Duke of Marlborough, the four-volume history of Britain called *A History of the English Speaking Peoples,* and even fiction. This was in addition to countless newspaper and journal articles. Churchill found a good agent and earned very high rewards for his writing. In fact, his writing was an economic necessity from his war correspondent work when it covered the expenses of a young officer, to later years when it paid for the upkeep of Chartwell and his family.

Justifiably, Churchill is most appreciated for his speeches. Certainly, he was a gifted orator, but the speeches were first written in clear and gripping prose, and he created images and swayed emotion in a style that was poetic, visceral, and stirring. Many of his most famous speeches have been alluded to in these pages and will have been familiar words even to those who did not know who had spoken them. His famous speeches were carefully crafted, practiced, and learned by heart, and he rarely spoke extempore.

In 1953, Churchill received the Nobel Prize for Literature, which particularly recognized his Marlborough biography. It was unusual for this to be awarded to a serving politician. It is to be supposed that his speeches, well known and ringing in the ears of the judges, also recommended him for this accolade.

# Chapter 9: The Legacy of Winston Churchill

In 2002, the people of the United Kingdom were invited to vote on who was the greatest Briton of all time. Churchill was the victor by a wide margin, beating William Shakespeare and Charles Darwin and, one supposes, Doctor Who and Sherlock Holmes. He still holds an iconic status as the preeminent statesman and leader who led the free world to victory over the evil tyrant Hitler. He personifies the ideal Englishman as described in Rudyard Kipling's poem "If-": "Meeting with triumph and disaster and treating those imposters just the same." After the war, he was spoken of with reverence by people of all political persuasions. In a million homes, there were dogs and parakeets named "Winston" in his honor by a grateful nation.

There is no question that he is an extraordinary figure in terms of his contributions to society on so many levels, including his ideas, his leadership qualities, and his dedication to duty. There will always be this to admire.

However, there are things about Churchill that are difficult for the contemporary, modern mind to accept. As an imperialist, he believed that a British (and white) civilization was superior to all other civilizations. He believed that there was a hierarchy of races and was in denial about the many wrongs done in the name of colonialism, focusing only on the British Empire's "gifts to the world." These views can be explained but never excused by the fact that they were typical of his era, class, and background.

On some issues, his record is contradictory. Churchill is, like many of his era, guilty of frequent, casual anti-Semitism but supported the Zionist cause and spoke against the mistreatment of Jews in Germany from the earliest days of Hitler's rise. While he believed that some races and societies were superior, he also believed that inhumanity and cruelty were abhorrent, thereby distinguishing himself from Hitler. His discourse on Islam is similarly contradictory.

Churchill made decisions and mistakes, especially in war, that some still question. He was in favor of using gas (tear gas, not mustard gas, in his mitigation) against the Kurds and Afghans who he described as "uncivilized tribes," defending himself that this was better than a dead British soldier in a trench, and that its use would ultimately limit loss of life.

Trades unionists will never forgive his treatment of striking miners in the early years of the 20th century, but they are neglectful to the fact that he spoke for minimum wages, worker's rights, better conditions, and a curb on mine owners' profits. Boris Johnson's biography of Churchill credits him with some of the "most progressive legislation for 200 years" and, controversially, considers him a founder of the welfare state in

Britain. In his post-war role as the Minister for Housing, he fulfilled his party's pledge of building 300,000 houses in a year. Could any politician manage that today?

When a person is accorded iconic status, they lose an acknowledgment of their human fallibility. Churchill was flawed and made mistakes. Some of his views were utterly indefensible. He is revered not just in the United Kingdom but across the world and continues to inspire many. Most agree that he defended freedom and democracy and was unafraid to be a lone voice and an object of derision until others came to see he was right.

Similarly, on a personal level, he could be rude and inconsiderate, even a bully, but he could also be kind and charming. He was eccentric and a bit of a maverick, which will always endear him to the British.

To understand Churchill, one must be able to hold these ambiguities and contradictions in equal measure.

Succeeding politicians have invoked Churchill throughout the years, including Margaret Thatcher when arguing for war against Argentina, and Tony Blair when defending the invasion of Iraq.

Footage of Churchill's funeral in 1965 is highly emotional. The smoggy streets of London were crowded with hundreds of thousands of ordinary people, some in tears (indeed, Labour Prime Minister Harold Winston is seen to be wiping a tear as is

Princess Margaret.) Queen Elizabeth II is there, even though it was not customary for monarchs to attend the funerals of commoners. The cranes situated on the docks of the East End lower in unison as his funeral barge passes. Without question, he was and is deeply loved.

# Conclusion

It would seem that Churchill still has a lot to teach us some 55 years after his death. The YouTube and Netflix generation will discover him in their own way. There have been many dramas made about his life, including *Darkest Hour* (Wright, 2017), starring Gary Oldman, which relates the events of 1940, and *The Gathering Storm* (Loncraine, 2002) that takes its audience from the wilderness years to the threshold of the Second World War and includes a touching portrait of Clementine and Winston's marriage. For those that would dive deeper, Richard Attenborough's film, *Young Winston* (Attenborough, 1972), follows Churchill from Harrow to the Boer War and then into Parliament. A TV series, *Jennie: Lady Randolph Churchill* (Cellan Jones, 1974), was made to coincide with the centenary of Churchill's birth. It tells the story of his beautiful, bright, and determined American mother.

Perhaps, Churchill's life is a particular inspiration as the world faces unprecedented challenges. We are all going to be needing grit and determination and a dose of Blitz Spirit in the coming years of economic challenges and new ways of living; we will need to summon our inner Churchill and "so bear ourselves" that others will say, "This was their finest hour..."

CPSIA information can be obtained
at www.ICGtesting.com
Printed in the USA
BVHW091234101121
621187BV00001B/112